Contents

Mechanic Mike says:
Tow trucks are also called breakdown trucks.

Mechanic Mike's Machines

Trucks

Franklin Watts
This edition published in the UK in 2016 by The Watts Publishing Group

Copyright © 2014 David West Children's Books

Designed and illustrated by David West

Dewey number 629.2'24
PB ISBN: 978 1 4451 5181 6

Printed in Malaysia

Franklin Watts
An imprint of
Hachette Children's Group
Part of The Watts Publishing Group
Carmelite House
50 Victoria Embankment
London EC4Y 0DZ

An Hachette UK Company.
www.hachette.co.uk

www.franklinwatts.co.uk

MECHANIC MIKE'S MACHINES TRUCKS
was produced for Franklin Watts by
David West Children's Books, 6 Princeton Court, 55 Felsham Road, London SW15 1AZ

Mechanic Mike says:
Mike will tell you something more about the machine.

ver
:hing you
know.

Is it fast or slow?
Top speeds are
given here.

What type of truck
is it, rigid body or
semi-trailer?

Get your
amazing
fact here!

Tow Truck

Tow trucks are used to tow away cars, buses and other vehicles that have broken down or have been badly damaged in an accident.

 The tow truck was invented in 1916 by an American called Ernest Holmes.

Although they have powerful engines their maximum speed is about 90 kilometres per hour.

 Did you know that companies that run **fleets** of trucks, such as fire brigades, have their own tow trucks?

These trucks are called **rigid body trucks**.

 Tow trucks need very powerful diesel engines to tow away even the largest vehicles.

Telescopic arm

Did you know that the **telescopic arm** on some mobile cranes can extend to 182 metres?

Mobile cranes use diesel engines to power the wheels and crane.

SCHWERLAST

SCHWERLAST

These trucks are rigid body trucks.

These monsters are slow. They travel at only 80 kilometres per hour.

Mobile cranes use **outriggers** that extend out from their sides and rest on the ground to make them more stable when they are using the crane.

Mobile Crane

These specialised trucks are used in the building industry. The crane uses its telescopic arm to lift heavy objects, such as steel girders, into place.

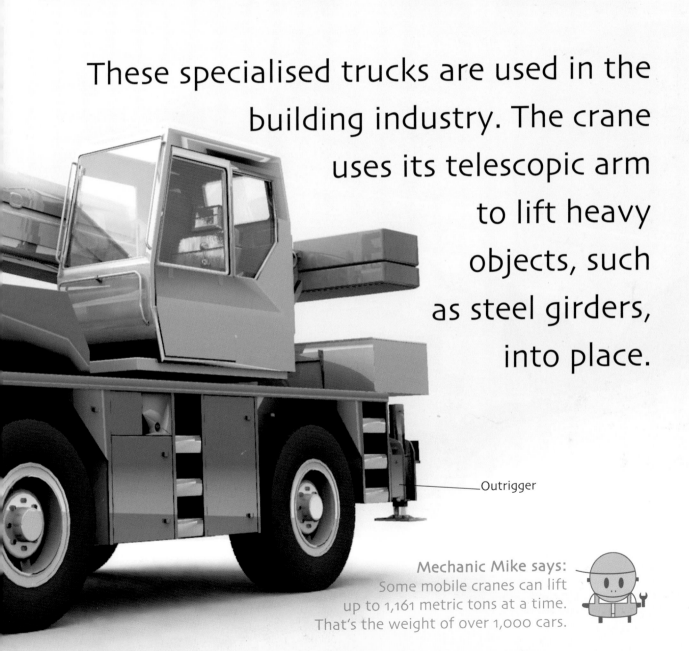

Outrigger

Mechanic Mike says:
Some mobile cranes can lift up to 1,161 metric tons at a time. That's the weight of over 1,000 cars.

The water hoses can pump 946 litres per minute.

Fire engines need to get to the fire fast! These trucks can travel at 120 kilometres per hour.

These trucks are rigid body trucks.

Did you know this pumper-tanker holds 3,785 litres of water?

Pumpers use diesel engines to power the wheels and the water pump.

Fire Engine

There are several types of fire engines. This is a pumper-tanker. It pumps water from its water tank, or from a **fire hydrant**, to hoses held by firefighters.

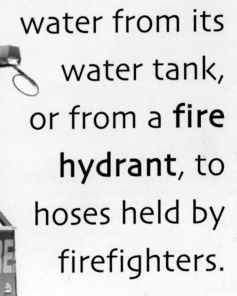

Mechanic Mike says: Fire engines are also called fire trucks.

Ambulances were first used on a battlefield by the French army in 1793. They were **horse-drawn** carriages.

 Ambulances need to get to the patient fast! They can travel at 129 kilometres per hour.

 These trucks are rigid body trucks.

 Did you know that even golf carts have been converted into ambulances?

 Most amulances use diesel engines.

Ambulance

These special trucks carry life-saving equipment. The driver uses sirens and flashing lights. These warn other drivers to get out of the way as the ambulance speeds to the rescue.

Mechanic Mike says:
Ambulances can also be motorbikes, cars, vans, boats, helicopters and planes (air ambulances).

Refrigerated Truck

Goods that may spoil, such as fish, meat and vegetables, can be transported long distances by road in a refrigerated truck.

Ice cream makers made one of the first refrigerated trucks in the late 1920s, for long-distance deliveries.

 These trucks have a speed of 112.7 kilometres per hour.

 This is a rigid body truck.

 These trucks use diesel engines to drive the rear wheels and supply power for the refrigeration unit.

 Many products need to be kept cool. Refrigerated trucks carry computers, photography and medical supplies, such as blood, as well as food and drinks.

Mechanic Mike says:
The first refrigerated cars were railway boxcars that were kept cool with ice cut from lakes and ponds in winter.

Concrete Mixer

Concrete is kept liquid in the turning drum of these large trucks as they deliver it to a building site. Once there, the concrete is poured out of the back.

Mechanic Mike says:
The inside of the drum on a concrete mixing truck is fitted with a spiral blade. When it turns one way it keeps the concrete in. When it turns in the opposite direction it forces the concrete out.

These trucks are also called cement mixers.

 They can carry about 18,100 kilogrammes of concrete, which is enough to fill a large room.

 Concrete mixers are limited to a speed of 90 kilometres per hour.

 These trucks are rigid body trucks.

 Concrete mixers use diesel engines.

Drum

CATERPILLAR

GOODYEAR

CAT

Mechanic Mike says:
These trucks have the largest tyres in the world at 4 metres high.

16

Dump Truck

These monsters do not travel on roads. They are designed to carry rock and soil at **open-cast mines** and large building sites.

These trucks are often transported in pieces and put together on site.

 They can carry up to about 363 metric tons. That's similar to 400 cars!

 These giants have a top speed of 64 kilometres per hour.

Giant trucks are rigid body trucks.

 A 20-cylinder diesel engine supplies electric power to the electric motors on each wheel.

Tanker

Tankers transport many different liquids such as milk, water, petrol, diesel and industrial chemicals.

Tractor unit

Large tanker trucks can carry between 21,000 to 34,000 litres. That's enough to fill a swimming pool.

Tanker trucks with a trailer that can be detached are called **semi-trailers**.

The top speed of these giant trucks is limited to 100 kilometres per hour.

This tanker is a semi-trailer truck.

These trucks use diesel engines to drive the wheels of the **tractor unit**.

Mechanic Mike says:
Tankers are also called tank trucks or road tankers.

Road Train

Road trains are trucks that carry large loads of freight in several wagons. They are used in remote areas of the world.

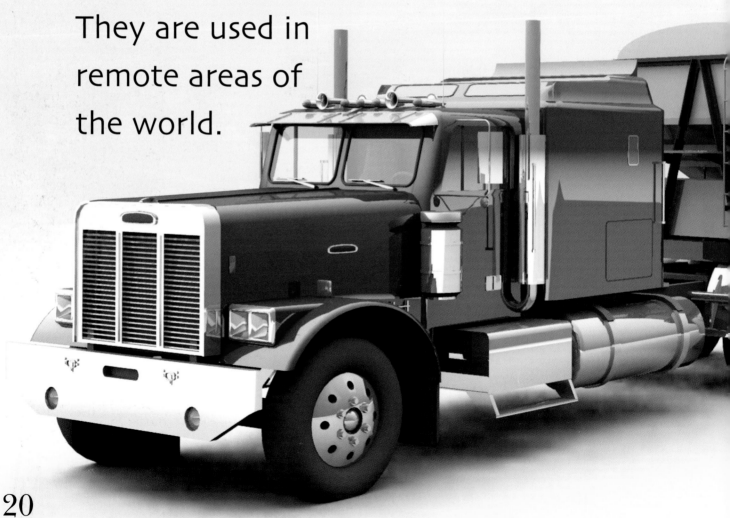

The record for the longest road train was 1.5 kilometres long. It only travelled 100 metres on a road in Australia to make the record!

Road trains can be seen in Argentina, Australia, Mexico, the United States and Canada.

These giants' top speed is limited to 100 kilometres per hour.

Road trains are semi-trailer trucks.

These trucks use powerful diesel engines to pull their massive weights.

Freight wagon

Mechanic Mike says:
The longest road trains operate in Australia. Trucks may tow as many as seven trailers.

Transporter

Transporters can carry all types of heavy loads from giant diggers to mining machinery. Even tanks can be carried on special army transporters.

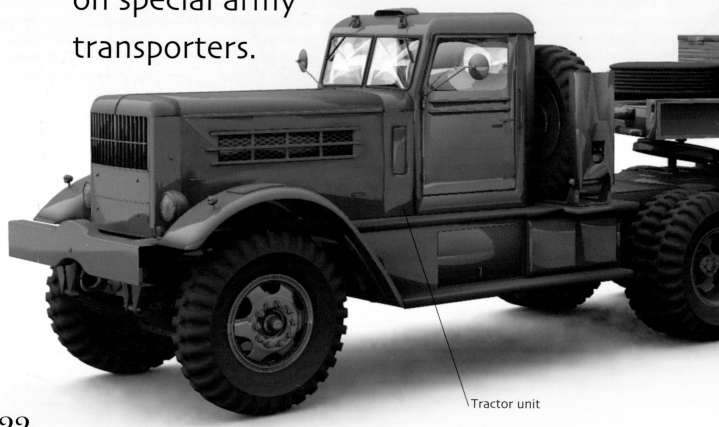

Tractor unit

Tank transporters carry main battle tanks that weigh 70.8 metric tons.

Tank transporters have a top speed of 80 kilometres per hour.

Transporters are semi-trailer trucks.

These trucks use powerful diesel engines to pull their heavy weights.

Some transporters are double-decked and can carry up to 12 cars.

Tank

Mechanic Mike says:
Transporting tanks to and from the battlefield, or during peacetime, is faster and saves the wear on the tanks' tracks.

Glossary

fire hydrant
A water outlet on a street.

fleets
Collections of vehicles owned by a company.

horse-drawn
Pulled by horses.

open-cast mine
An area of land dug into to extract coal or ore.

outrigger
A mechanical arm that extends out and rests on the ground as a stabiliser.

rigid body truck
A truck with a tractor unit and a separate goods unit.

semi-trailer
A truck made up of a tractor unit and a removable trailer unit.

telescopic arm
A mechanical arm that can get longer or shorter.

tractor unit
The part of a truck that has the engine and cab.

Index